Old TINTO VILLAGES
by

Ann Matheson

Although this photograph was taken outside the Horse Market stance in Lanark, the 'Tinto' bus belonged to Plenderleith of Symington who operated the Lanark-Biggar route in the 1920s. The bus is a 14-seater Dennis, the driver Robert Cranston and the conductor Bert Bruce.

Text © Ann Matheson 1998
First Published in the United Kingdom, 1998, reprinted 2008
by Stenlake Publishing Limited,
54-58 Mill Square, Catrine, KA5 6RD
01290 551122
www.stenlake.co.uk

ISBN 9781840330397

ACKNOWLEDGEMENTS

Brian Lambie; Margaret Murphy, Hamilton Library; Martain Brown;
Tam Ward; William Brownlie. The picture on page 1 is reproduced
by courtesy of Robert Grieves. The picture on page 21 is reproduced
by courtesy of Jimmy Graham. The picture on page 36 is reproduced
by courtesy of Janet Rae. With the exception of the above and those
on the inside front cover and pages 1, 9, 11, 15, 16, 18, 20, 22, 23, 24,
26, 28, 29, 30, 31, 32, 34, 37, 38 and 47, all pictures are reproduced by
courtesy of Biggar Museum Trust.

Situated about 1 km north of the present day village, the sixteenth
century Lamington Tower may have been built on the motte where
Lambin, the Flemish founder of the settlement, had his fortified
homestead in the twelfth century. Members of the Braidfute family,
who held Lamington Castle for Scotland in the Wars of Independence,
were slaughtered there by Hasilrig, the Sheriff of Lanark, and his men.
Blind Harry's narrative tells the tragic tale of Marion Braidfute, who
was abducted and later became the 'leman' (sweetheart) of Wallace.
Her own barbarous death, also at the hands of Hasilrig, allegedly led
to Wallace's vow to devote himself to the service of his country:

> To thee I swear, this sword I'll never sheath
> Till I revenge my dearest, dearest's death. (Blind Harry's *Wallace*)

The tower was dismantled by the Lamington Estate factor at the end
of the eighteenth century, partly by the use of gunpowder. Some of its
carved stones were used as lintels on neighbouring farm buildings.
Since this picture was taken most of the remaining tower has collapsed.

INTRODUCTION

The villages which now form a necklace around the base of Tinto are, historically speaking, recent foundations dating only from the twelfth century. For over 7,000 years before that, successive waves of settlers peopled the area, leaving behind a landscape rich in archaeological remains, romance and legend.

The earliest of these were nomadic Stone Age hunters and gatherers whose stone implements have been found throughout the upper Clyde valley. Bronze Age people (2000 BC - 600 BC) built the enormous cairn on Tinto's summit, from which Goat Fell in Arran and the peaks of Cumbria can be seen on a clear day. At this vantage point, beacon fires would have been lit, perhaps earning the hill the name Tintock or *teinteach*, 'place of fire'. These people buried their dead in cairns on Tinto's foothills and ornaments of finely beaten gold found at Coulter tell of the sophistication of their society. The people of the Iron Age (600 BC - AD 400) lived in circular hill-top forts, fortified with ramparts and ditches which can still be seen; for example at Quothquan Law, Cow Castle near Coulter, or Fallburn, beside the footpath to Tinto's summit. At Green Knowe, on the wet lands near Coulter, these Iron Age people built a crannog or lake dwelling. The Roman legions who first invaded the area in AD 79 left behind a temporary camp beside the Clyde at Cornhill, a stopover point on their route from the Clyde Valley to their major camp at Carstairs. St Ninian's Mission, dating from the fifth century, is recorded in a cluster of place names, for example St Ninian's Chapel and Well at Lamington as well as the ancient chapels at Wiston and Warrenhill in Covington parish.

Most of today's villages were named after the Flemings who founded them in the twelfth century. These Flemings were a branch of the Normans, some of whom filtered north into Scotland after the Norman Conquest of England. Thus Thankerton, Wiston, Covington, Lamington and Symington were the lands belonging to – or *tons* – of Tancard, Wice, Colban, Lambin and Symon Loccard. They received their lands from the king in exchange for military support. The place names Quothquan and Coulter are etymologically more elusive, the former perhaps meaning 'a water course by the hill' and the latter a 'narrow stretch of land'. These Fleming overlords built defensive castles on artificial mounds or mottes. Some of these mottes can still be seen and the sites of others perhaps traced from names like 'The Place' in Wiston and Symington. While most mottes were later abandoned in favour of larger stone castles elsewhere, in Lamington a castle may have been built on the existing motte. Here, in the thirteenth century, according to the poet Blind Harry, lived Marion Braidfute, the 'wife' of William Wallace, whose legend lingers on in many local place names. Wallace's Seat on Quothquan Law was allegedly the spot where he conferred with his advisers, and the so-called Wallace's Sword was found in Covington parish.

Defensive homes were essential in succeeding centuries when reiving (cattle raiding) was a way of life, and the lawless Lindsays of Covington earned themselves a reputation in rhyme:

> Who rides so fast down the Coulter braes
> The Devil, or a Lindsay?

Less wealthy farmers, who could not afford thick-walled towers, built bastle houses with vaulted basements and barred windows, like Windgate in Cowgill Glen. Up to the end of the eighteenth century ordinary folk lived in tiny hamlets or 'fermtouns' of six to eight houses. Many present day farms, like Sorn Falla and Drumalbyn on Tinto's southern slopes, were fermtouns, whose poignant runrigs (ridge and furrow strips of land) could be clearly seen snaking down Tinto's lower slopes up to the late 1980s when they were obliterated by forestry.

The eighteenth and early nineteenth centuries saw the Tinto villages established as self-sufficient communities, with economies based on agriculture and some handloom weaving. Most saw a sharp decline in population during the Lowland Clearances of the late eighteenth and early nineteenth centuries, when farm enclosures and mechanisation created rural unemployment and former arable land was turned over to sheep grazing. Factory-produced textiles killed off the weaving industry at almost the same time. The coming of the railways in 1848 brought the first commuters, who caught the Tinto Express to their work in Glasgow. The same train brought holiday-makers to the area, bringing about the creation of local golf courses and the building of holiday homes for the summer visitors.

Today, although the local stations are closed, the villages remain as dormitory settlements and the area retains its many attractions for those who seek 'recreation' in its fullest sense.

In 1837 Alexander Baillie Cochrane, who became the first Lord Lamington in 1883, inherited the Lamington estate from his mother. Finding it in a dilapidated condition he instituted ambitious schemes, redeveloping Lamington as a 'model village' and building Lamington House in the Elizabethan style. The house was extended annually until by 1858 it had 58 rooms; a ball was held that year for 200 guests to inaugurate 'the extensive suite of rooms lately added to the mansion'. The stylish grounds contained a private Episcopalian chapel, Holy Trinity (1857). Various relatives and friends contributed gifts to embellish its interior, including the pulpit of Caen stone and the first stained glass windows to be seen in the district since the Reformation. Above the porch was a cross from the Appian Way. Trinity Chapel was adopted by Biggar Museum Trust in the 1980s, and in 1997 the first wedding for over 75 years took place there. In 1895 Alexander Cochrane's son Wallace (named after Sir William) became Governor General of Queensland, where his wife's tea-cakes, known as 'Lamingtons', have since become part of Australian culinary culture. The last Lord Lamington died in 1951 with no male heirs, and two years later the 'big hoose' was demolished. Its ruins were cleared away in 1980.

This tree with its surrounding seat, photographed in 1910, was a Lamington landmark until 1947. It was a village custom for boys aspiring to manhood to attempt to hurl a big stone over the lowest projecting tree limb. The stone had a ring attached to it, serving as a handle, and was kept under the tree. Two other notable Lamington 'seats' were the so-called Wallace's Chair and the 'canty' (repentance stool), both of which were to be found in Lamington Kirk. The former, allegedly from Lamington Tower, was gifted to the church by Lord Lamington in 1951. The canty was one of the last in use in Scotland, only discarded in 1828 when the church was refurbished.

Lamington Glen, through which the Lamington Burn flows north-west to join the River Clyde, was laid out by Alexander Baillie Cochrane as a planned rural retreat. Here he planted trees and built rustic bridges, sheltered pathways and heather-thatched huts like the one in the picture. There was also a landscaped duck pond. The writer of the *New Statistical Account* (1841) reported that hares, blackcock, grouse and partridge were plentiful in the area, adding that although otter numbers had declined, the corncraik could still be heard in summer.

In 1847 Lady Lamington and the Countess of Home established a school for girls, which was relocated in the village in 1868 when the Lamington family purchased the rest of the estate from the Homes. At the same time a cottage was built for the teacher, who taught reading, writing, geography and needlework. The village library, comprising several hundred volumes, was also housed in Lady Lamington's School, which was transferred to the School Board in 1912. The village's second parish school opened in 1877. Behind the class of 1914 is the kirkyard of Lamington Church. Built in 1721 on the site of the former St Ninian's Church, the kirk incorporates a fine twelfth century doorway. When Robert Burns visited in 1789 or 1791 he engraved a less than flattering piece of graffiti on the window:

As cauld a wind as ever blew
A caulder kirk and in't but few:
As cauld a minister's e'er spak,
Ye'se a' be het ere I come back.

In 1715 200 Highland soldiers retreating from the English border were brought down from the hills above Lamington and boarded overnight in Lamington church, before being despatched to Lanark. Biggar Museum Trust now owns the kirk, the east end of which is used as a studio by Crear McCartney, the stained glass artist.

In the mid-nineteenth century, carriers and hucksters carried on a healthy trade collecting and delivering locally produced butter, skim milk, buttermilk, sweet milk cheese and turkeys. Working Clydesdales such as these were a far cry from the horses that participated in the famous eighteenth century Lamington Races, held on the flat holms beside the Clyde. The identity of this carrier, photographed in Lamington *c.*1910, is unknown.

Castlehill Poultry Farm, Symington, Lanarkshire.

This poultry farm, part of Castlehill Farm, was situated on the northern slopes of Castlehill. The hill's tree-crowned summit still bears the traces of circular ramparts and ditches, built as defences for an Iron Age fort, one of many in the area. Castlehill Farmhouse, which has been home to members of the Lean family for several generations, can be seen far right. In 1841 Symington parish was recorded as being home to 106 families, 40 of whom were engaged in agriculture and 42 in trade, manufactures or handicrafts. The building of the Carlisle to Stirling road in the 1830s gave agriculture – and particularly dairy farming – a stimulus by providing speedier access to the market at Lanark. At the time Castlehill operated as a general farm but subsequently specialised. As well as poultry farming, it was one of the first places in the area where glasshouses were built for tomato growing. In the 1930s the Symington schoolmaster, William McCormack, used to release pupils from their studies to dig leaf mould from Castlehill woods as compost for the school garden.

During the First World War, sphagnum moss was collected for use in making dressings. This picture shows Symington schoolchildren, supervised by teacher Mr Hamilton, and Mrs Norrie, a summer visitor, with their contributions to the war effort.

Village Green, Old Symington

The whitewashed cottages with thatched roofs and small low windows are typical weavers' cottages, built in the early and mid-nineteenth century when handloom weaving was integral to the village's economy. In 1851 the 37 weavers, 1 lint spinner and 11 cotton throwsters who threaded the looms represented more than half the work-force; a work-force whose livelihood was destroyed when cheap factory-produced cotton became available in the later nineteenth century. Here, on the Green, villagers used to play quoits and hold their shows and fairs. It was also the place where they lit their Hogmanay bonfire. The nineteenth century school and schoolhouse were on the north side of the green.

Symington's village library was near the foot of Wellbrae, the site of the most reliable well in the district. In 1910 this old thatched building was succeeded by a new public library and village hall. Two drums were kept in this hall, one of which had formerly been used to rouse the weavers for their early morning shift.

Most of these houses on the south-facing side of Clyde Street (now Main Street) were built in the nineteenth century. About 200m north is 'The Place', probably the site of Symon Loccard's defensive castle (Loccard was the twelfth century Flemish founder of Symington). Symington Post Office, photographed *c.*1900, was also known as Drumelzier. Although it has been demolished and replaced by a modern bungalow, other buildings in the picture have changed remarkably little in a century. Letters posted at Drumelzier were stamped Symington while those sent from the post office at the western end of the village were franked New Symington.

Two storey 'modern' terraces, built just before the First World War, represent 'New Symington' at the western end of the village. One of the Prentice girls stands at the door of the well-stocked shop; the man with the horse is Bill Prentice. Mason's the butcher's shop is the present day post office.

This postcard was sent to Mrs T. Russell of Hawthorne Cottage, Lesmahagow, in June 1912. The message from 'P' reads: 'You might send on my old trousers as I am in the cook house'. In the early 1900s the Symington district was a popular site for yeomanry camps. This picture shows the present A72, just east of the railway bridge in Symington. The old Hartree Arms, known by locals as the Cleekum Inn, was built to the right of the bridge. Originally named after Dickson Hartree, a director of the Caledonian Railway, the inn later became the station-master's house.

Railway Station, Symington.

326

Symington Station was built at an important junction, where the Symington, Biggar and Peebles branch line joined the main north-south Caledonian line. The opening of the Caledonian Railway in 1848 brought the first commuters to the area, and marked the beginning of Symington's short life as a holiday resort. A goods shed and Jackson's slaughterhouse, which supplied Smithfield, stood beside the station. The 'meat train' arrived at 10.25 a.m. to be loaded up by 12.30 for a speedy journey south. In 1982 the slaughterhouse was closed and the site sold to Biggar Auction Mart Co. Ltd. Queen Elizabeth arrived by royal train at Symington to open the Daer Water Scheme in 1956. Passenger services came to an end in 1965.

Japanese influence is apparent in the ornamental gardens, pagoda and bridge of Lochan Tui. The loch was originally the reservoir where water was stored to drive the wheel at Symington Mill. It was enlarged and landscaped by the owner, Raeburn Mann, one of three proprietors who built large villas in Camps Wood as holiday homes. For this reason local people always called it 'Mann's Pond' rather than using the more fanciful name of Lochan Tui. In the thirties youngsters used to skate on the pond, where the low arch of the Japanese bridge was a challenging obstacle.

A nineteenth century writer likened Tinto to a 'brooding sphinx', overshadowing the surrounding landscape. Smoothed and rounded by Ice Age glaciers, Tinto is an igneous intrusion, made of magma which forced its way up from the earth's molten interior but did not break through the surface. This picture was taken from Castlehill. The train steaming north to Symington is about to pass the gable end of Westside Cottage, beyond which is the old Carlisle Road, now the A73, which, like the railway line, follows the Clyde Valley route south through the Southern Uplands. The writer of this postcard, dated 14 August 1912, complains of the bitter cold but records: 'Had a splendid run to Windermere – left about 5.45 a.m. and got home at 12 midnight. But a day on the lakes was worth it'.

Symington Golf Club was established in response to the development of the village as a holiday resort. The club closed in the 1930s and the pavilion, which was opposite the present Tinto Garage, was later used as a Scout hut before being relocated beside the Clyde as a shelter/summer house for anglers. John McInnes, who was the buyer for Jackson's slaughterhouse, is on the right of this 1910 photograph, with William Brown in the centre. The rather ethereal figure in the background is Sarah Carse (later Rae), daughter of a local builder. The beech tree in the background lives on.

Symington Lodge, a thatched folly, was one of the properties attached to the neo-Georgian Symington House. The last of the 'big hooses' in the area, this was built by Andrew Prentice in 1915. The lodge, which had all mod cons for its day, still stands, now with slates replacing the thatch.

Tinto Vale, at the north-west end of Main Street, was the home of John Plenderleith. These new cars, photographed *c.*1924, are a splendid advertisement for the Tinto Garage. The drivers are John Plenderleith, Frank Graham and, in the left-hand drive vehicle, David Learmonth from Lochmaben. To the right of the house is J.&J. Plenderleith's first joinery shop. In pre-electricity days, the saw was operated by water-wheel, the water being led from a nearby pond, the site of which can still be seen. Water was fed into this pond through an aqueduct under the road at what was called the 'Iron Brig' about 100 yards from the post office. The iron bridge sides were about five feet high and Jimmy Graham, who spent his youth in Symington, recalls that their panels were 'ideal for circus posters' which remained stuck to them long after the circuses made their occasional visits to the village.

Castledykes Smithy, church and manse, Wiston. Wiston was the largest of several fermtouns on the lower south-facing slopes of Tinto, where good drainage and the sunny aspect provided the conditions needed for successful crop growing. The runrig (ridge and furrow) system was still in use in 1793 when the first *Statistical Account* was written. Castledykes (above), on the present A73 at the north end of the village, may have been the site of twelfth century mottes, although settlement in the Wiston area dates to much earlier times. In 1967 two Bronze Age cairns were excavated near Newton of Wiston. They contained the remains of twelve bodies, including burials in cists and cremations in urns, as well as grave goods and flint remains. The former church, which dates from 1886 and is now a private house, has very fine art nouveau style stained glass windows made by Stephen Adam and Son, a Glasgow partnership of 1893-1904. The round churchyard, which may date to pre-Christian times, is almost completely encircled by an earth rampart about six feet high. It contains early eighteenth century tombstones, some with carvings denoting the occupations of the deceased.

WISTON MILL & MARSHLANDS.

The mill at the southern end of Wiston was driven by water from a lade cut from the Garf Water. The same lade served a lint mill further west. The photographer was facing south-west towards the farm at Marchlands.

THE SHOP, WISTON.

This building, photographed in the late 1920s, still exists, but has not been a 'Jenny a' Things' shop since the 1970s.

Most folk are familiar with the enigmatic Tinto rhyme, of unknown origins:

> On Tintock tap there is a mist
> And in that mist there is a kist
> And in that kist there is a caup
> And in that caup there is a drap.
> Tak up that caup, drink aff the drap
> And set the caup on Tintock Tap.

On Tintock Tap

The picture shows what is probably a Bronze Age cairn, dating back about 3,500 years. The cairn, 45m wide and 6m high, is continually added to by climbers who contribute their own stones to the mound. On 9 September 1958, Tinto was climbed by an Austin 'Gipsy' carrying a brass plate which was to be cemented to the viewfinder at the summit. Fitted with land-grip tyres, the truck took one-and-a-half hours to make the ascent.

Covington Church. Colban, the founder of Covington, received his lands from King Malcolm IV in 1189. In 1296 Hurve de Chastel-Bernard, the parson of the church of Colbanstoun, swore fealty to Edward I, as did Margaret and Isabelle de Colbanstoun. When Robert the Bruce gained the crown he confiscated the Colban lands and gave them to Keith, Marischal of Scotland. In the fifteenth century they passed from his family to the Lindsays. Covington Tower, on the extreme right, dates from 1420-1440 and was built by the Lindsays within the defences of the earlier medieval moated site, possibly the remains of Colban's twelfth century 'castle'. The three metre thick tower walls contained a dungeon and garderobe (privy). In 1525 Lindsay, rector of Colbintoune, and his relative, the lord of the manor, were accused of being party to the murder of Weir of Stanebyres.

UNVEILING CARGILL MONUMENT, THANKERTON 8TH JULY 1911.

Donald Cargill, the Covenanter, preached his last sermon at Dunsyre Common in 1681. He left the moor after darkness fell, knowing that his enemies were anxious to claim the 500 merks offered by the government for his capture, and went to spend the night at Covington Mill. There, along with Walter Smith and William Boig, he was captured by James Irvine of Bonshaw, a dealer in horses, who had received a commission to hunt down all who attended Conventicles. Irvine took his prisoners to Lanark Tolbooth, from where they were transferred to Edinburgh. In July 1681 they were found guilty of high treason, hanged, and their heads placed on the Nether Bow. A short time later Irvine was killed in a drunken brawl in Lanark. The monument, erected by Covington Church's Bible Class and their friends, was unveiled on 8 July 1911.

COVINGTON MAINS FARM, WHERE BURNS STOPPED ON HIS WAY TO EDINBURGH 1786.

BRANDON SERIES.

The original farmhouse, on the right, no longer exists. Here Burns spent a night in 1786 when it was the home of Archibald Prentice, whose son, also called Archibald, later became the founder and editor of the *Manchester Times*. He recalled the excitement of Burns's visit, when a sheet attached to a pitchfork and stuck on top of a cornstack announced the famous guest's arrival to neighbouring farmers. Burns, on his way to Edinburgh from Mossgiel to publish the second edition of his poems, seems to have wooed the Covington agricultural community with as much charm as he did the Edinburgh gentry. He later described the evening as 'a most agreeable little party'. On the morning following his stay, while his pony was shod by the local blacksmith, he had a very leisurely breakfast at Hillhead Farm, lasting the whole forenoon. Archibald Prentice was sufficiently enthusiastic about Burns's poetry to subscribe for twenty copies of the Edinburgh edition.

The grandiose plans for Carmichael House never came to fruition. Built in 1734 by the Third Earl of Hyndford, just behind the site of a medieval 'castle', the house was supposed to have an elaborate frontage, but only the north and south wings and a connecting corridor were completed. The Third Earl was an eminent statesman who had been ambassador to Prussia, Russia and Vienna. He held the post of Vice-Admiral of Scotland from 1752 to 1764, and was one of the early 'improvers', carrying out extensive schemes to enclose the estate land and plant avenues and gardens. Carmichael House is now a ruin and in 1997 the stone eagles, which were a local landmark, were stolen from the gates at the entrance to the drive.

The distinctive pyramid of Quothquan Law (335m), the site of one of many Iron Age forts in the area, overlooks Thankerton. Thankerton owes its name to the Fleming Tancard, who received the lands from King Malcolm IV in the twelfth century. Like most of the Tinto villages, Thankerton's economy was dominated by agriculture and weaving up to the mid-nineteenth century when the arrival of the railways brought great changes to a village that was then a cluster of thatched cottages and occasional farms. The large stone villas were built between the 1850s and 1920s for commuters who travelled daily to Glasgow on the Tinto Express. The waggons on wheels are railwaymen's huts, part of the moveable furniture of the goods yard.

Clyde from boat Farm, Thankerton

This postcard was sent by a holiday-maker staying at Aldersyde, Thankerton, in July 1909. The lush grassland beside the Clyde was ideally suited for dairy cattle. In 1975 a Bronze Age burial cist containing the skeletons of a woman, a child and an unusually tall young man, buried in a crouched position with a beaker alongside the body, were found during gravel quarrying near Boat Farm. These remains were dated to *c*.1780 BC. The ferry across the Clyde at this point (from which the farm derives its name), became surplus to requirements when Thankerton Bridge was built by public subscription in 1778. In the late nineteenth century, a horse and cart disappeared near here while excavating gravel. Locals have since referred to the area as 'The Horse Hole'.

Townhead, Thankerton from the Station.

The coming of the railways in 1848 made Thankerton into a popular Victorian holiday destination. Holiday-makers often stayed in the low-roofed weavers' cottages, although their thatch was susceptible to being set alight by sparks from the engines. Thankerton women caught the Tinto Express to Glasgow and allegedly took aspirins prior to their arrival to prepare them for a day's shopping in the city! Regrettably, the Tinto Express made its last run in December 1964; the station was closed to passengers on 4 January 1965. This postcard, with the announcement 'Central Station Hotel, Glasgow, Now Open', dates from before the building of the creamery. In the 1960s a bowling green was laid out in the field between Sherrifflatts Road and the signal box.

RAILWAY SMASH AT THANKERTON. 6/2/08.

At 1.45 a.m. on 6 February 1908 several waggons of a heavy goods train from Carlisle left the line at Thankerton . By 7.45 a.m. the breakdown gang had managed to clear one line to allow traffic through. Amazingly, no-one was injured and, although the mail was several hours late, normal services had been resumed by 4 p.m.

Located by the station, the creamery, built in 1911, was ideally placed to despatch fresh dairy produce from the surrounding farms to urban markets in both the east and west. On its opposite side, a long loading ramp led from Sherrifflatts Road to the first floor where there were double doors, replaced by windows when the ramp was removed. Although the creamery ceased operation in the 1930s, the buildings remain as a depot for industrial refrigerators.

Thankerton's 9 hole golf course had a superb location on the gently sloping banks of the Clyde between Boat Farm and Muirhouse Farm. It was opened on 10 June 1905 by Captain Thomas Carmichael, the Laird of Eastend. The Rev. Mr MacGregor, who presided at the opening ceremony, suggested that one of the reasons for the popularity of golf was that 'it was not confined to the lords of creation, but ladies could and did join in the game'. Here, to demonstrate the point, Lady Anstruther Carmichael drives the first ball using a club with which she was presented on the occasion. The Haskell golf ball, in a glass case, has now found its way into the collection of Biggar Museum Trust!

Cormiston Estate, about 2 km east of Thankerton, lies on gently sloping land north of the sharp bend in the Clyde at Wolfclyde Bridge, the more distant of the two bridges in the background. Only the piers now remain of the nearer railway bridge, built in 1864 to carry the Symington, Biggar and Broughton railway line. The track was lifted in 1966 when the line was closed. This lively harvest scene was captured in the late nineteenth century. Since then, Netherton House has been built (1910) between Cormiston and the Clyde at this point.

SHIELDHILL.

The Chancellors of Shieldhill seem to have come from France at the time of the Norman Conquest of England in 1066. Hugo Cancellarius witnessed the signature of William I of Scotland in 1199. The family seems to have had two residences, the earlier of these at Shieldhill, since it is recorded that they were forced to return to Shieldhill after the Regent Moray razed their residence at 'Quodquan' to the ground, following their support for Mary Queen of Scots at the Battle of Langside in 1567. This residence may have been on the site of the old row of cottages known as 'The Castle' at Shieldhill Mains. The twelfth century tower of Shieldhill now forms the entrance to the present Shieldhill House Hotel. The spiral staircase within the thick walls led to a private chapel with a slit in the wall to provide light and ventilation to a hiding place that probably dates from the period of Roman Catholic persecution. The family certainly fell foul of the local minister in the seventeenth century when Robert Chancler was accused of railing against his pastor and his daughter of 'burying a bairne's claithes for to procure health'. When Lady Chancellor died in 1639, Robert Chancellor buried her secretly in the church, because the pastor would not permit this 'superstitious Popish practice'. The Lady in Grey is a well-known ghost which haunts the staircase and passages.

Quothquan

Between 1778 and 1793, 25 cottages in Libberton and Quothquan parish were pulled down and only three new ones built. The minister of the time blamed absentee landlords for the depopulation of the parish, arguing that had they occupied their estates they would have provided employment for both agricultural and domestic workers. Increasing mechanisation in the first half of the twentieth century exacerbated the trend of depopulation, which was particularly marked during the Depression years of the 1920s and 30s. By 1951, all the former weavers' cottages at Quothquan were gone. Huntfield Place, above, replaced a row of old houses known as 'The Castle'. In 1898 the six houses in the row were converted to four, the outside stairs removed and an upper storey added to the east end. This was subsequently extended along the whole length of the row.

Although there are several large estates in the vicinity of Coulter (spelled Culter in old maps and descriptions), the village itself is dominated by the early nineteenth century mill, which has been a hotel since 1990. Low handloom weavers' cottages and later two-storey houses are grouped loosely round the mill, which was still operating when this picture was taken in the late nineteenth century. The motte at Wolfclyde was the twelfth century stronghold of Alexander de Cutir, but the Bronze Age finds in this area, as well as several notable Iron Age forts and cultivation terraces, testify to a settlement period that goes back at least 4,000 years.

This stone-built terrace replaced a row of estate cottages, similar to those still visible on the far left of this 1900 picture. At the time Coulter was a self-sufficient community with its own smithy, mill, tailor, cobbler, dyker, ditcher, thatcher and joiner. By 1951, only the joiner's shop remained. Flax for linen was grown, processed and woven in the village up to the late nineteenth century.

The minister of 1793 observed that the lack of a bridge over the Coulter Water was a severe handicap to the village, since the ford was often impassable. As the district was short of peat mosses, the distance from coal supplies– eleven miles away in Douglas– was a serious problem in winter. At one time parishioners also complained that the parish church 'on the other side of a great river... was seldom accessible to them without danger '. Since the 'great river' referred to was the Coulter Water, one suspects that their religious fervour was a little lukewarm! These problems were no doubt solved when the bridge, which carries the A702 from Edinburgh to Dumfries over the burn, was built in the 1830s. The parapet was removed in 1951 and further alterations made in 1982.

The lands of Coulter Maynes were held by the Brown family for over 300 years from the fifteenth century. In 1571, John Brown of Coulter Maynes had to forfeit his holdings to Mary Queen of Scots because of his support for the Lennox faction, but they were later restored. Another John Brown was called before the Presbytery of Biggar in 1646 to confess to having secretly aided Montrose during Charles I's reign. In 1817, the property was acquired by David Sim whose son Adam, a notable antiquarian, built a new mansion in 1839 on the site of the original house. In this picture, taken in 1952, the new mansion is seen through the portals of the old, which now form the entrance to the garden. The new house had one apartment roofed with oak panels from Glasgow Cathedral, and two ceilings were painted in water-colour by the Italian artist, Prioli, in 1857. Adam Sim filled the house with antiquities, including 100 editions of the Bible, the keystone of Glasgow Bridge and the gold-laced skull cap worn by Charles I at his execution.

The VA prefix on the bike signifies that it was registered in Lanarkshire. Dora Don, the bike's owner, was then the teacher at Coulter School. The old school, now the kitchen of the village hall, is visible in the background behind the new school house.

Among the pupils photographed outside Coulter School in 1914 are David Finlayson, looking jaunty in his cap, and his sister Janet, second from the right in the front row: the teacher is Joseph Walker. The present Coulter Primary School was built when the old school, inset, was closed in 1911. In the nineteenth century Greek, Latin, maths and geography were taught in addition to the three Rs. David Sim of Coulter Maynes, who died in London in 1834, mortified £100 for 'the education and clothing of a boy or girl in the parish of Coulter, of industrious parents'.

Shepherds at Culter Waterhead in the 1880s with traditional plaids over their shoulders. Up to the twentieth century, these were made in Coulter parish from local wool, and finished by the local tailor. They were folded into a 'plaid-neuk' to create a carrying place for lambs. In the nineteenth century, at East Mains, about 1 km north-east of Coulter, there was a hamlet of five cottages where agriculture and weaving were practised on a communal basis. Apparently other activities were too, since it is recorded that on Sunday mornings the men gathered at the common spigot to wash before going to church. Although the only shepherds firmly identified are Jimmy Scott, who is standing on the extreme right, and Ben Mundell (centre front), shepherds at Coulter in the 1881 census included Robert Anderson, William Melrose, William Anderson, William Smail, Andrew Anderson and William Stevenson.

Richard Brown of Hartree is mentioned in a deed recorded at Lanark in 1409. The tower of Hartree stood on a defensive knoll surrounded by marshland not far from Hartree House, which has been a hotel since 1948. The old tower was demolished in the late eighteenth century when this mansion was built by Colonel Alexander Dickson, whose family obtained the estate in 1630. Here, the Lindsay brothers and their work-force are grouped as if for an advertisement during redecoration work in 1880, when considerable extensions were made to the house. Walter Lindsay is in the centre of the picture and his twin brother John on the extreme right. In the 1930s, Hartree was a private school for boys, whose outfits had to include, among other items, '6 Eton collars, 2 tweed suits, 1 kilt suit or dark suit and 2 military hair brushes in case'. During the Second World War, Edinburgh Academy pupils were evacuated to Hartree, and in 1947 Hartree Arts Club, the forerunner of Biggar Music Club, held concerts in the 'studio'.

Around the turn of the century, reservoirs were built at Cowgill and Culter Waterhead: the former for Airdrie and Coatbridge Water Company, completed in 1899; the latter for Motherwell, completed in 1907. This is the temporary village built for the workers at Culter Waterhead. The canteen was to the left of the track; the school, mission house, reading room, grocery store and navvies' huts to the right. The canteen was open only in the evenings and the liquor strictly rationed! On top of the embankment in the middle distance are two narrow gauge locomotives, one with tip trucks and the other with a low sided waggon. The final embankment was over 26m high, retaining a lake 1 km long with a 2,275 million litre capacity. When Lord Lamington officially opened a hall at Cowgill Waterworks, built in 1895 by private subscription to provide recreation for the navvies, he rather patronisingly claimed he had heard good accounts of the men and 'not a single rabbit was missing'.

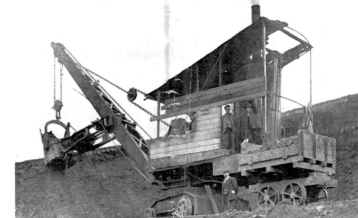

Puddle clay was essential for filling the trench in the earth embankments of these reservoirs to render them watertight. To transport suitable clay and other materials to Culter Waterhead, a 12 km single track railway line was built to connect with the Caledonian Railway system. This line ran parallel to the present A702 from Causewayend, Biggar, through to the waterhead, past Culter Allers Farm and along the service road that had been built in 1903. The upper photograph shows Robert McAlpine's Hudswell Clarke engine leaving Causewayend sidings. Alongside it are the Caledonian Railway's horse and cart from Biggar. The reservoir was completed in 1907, despite frequent delays brought about by bad weather. Heavy snowfalls and hard frosts made working with both concrete and clay impossible. The other picture, also taken from a brochure detailing the engineering works, is captioned '12-ton steam navvy, employed to excavate material for embankment'.